Strange Creatures That Really Lived

Strange Creatures

by **Millicent Selsam**

illustrations by Jennifer Dewey

That Really Lived

SCHOLASTIC INC.

New York   Toronto   London   Auckland   Sydney

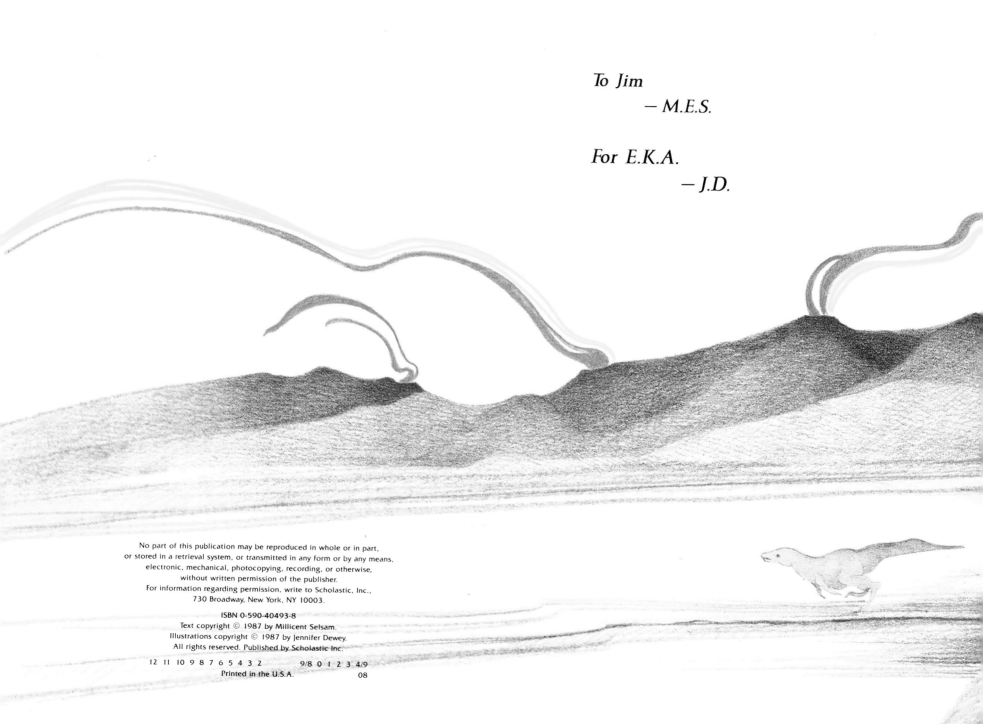

To Jim
— M.E.S.

For E.K.A.
— J.D.

ISBN 0-590-40493-8
Text copyright © 1987 by Millicent Selsam.
Illustrations copyright © 1987 by Jennifer Dewey.
All rights reserved. Published by Scholastic Inc.

12 11 10 9 8 7 6 5 4 3 2   9/8 0 1 2 3 4/9
Printed in the U.S.A.   08

Strange animals have always lived on Earth.

Some, like the dinosaurs, lived on land.

Other queer animals lived in the sea.
Some looked like fish,
and some looked like lizards.
Others looked like turtles with very long necks.

Strange-looking animals flew through the air, too.

One of the largest of the flying animals was the *pteranodon* (ter-<u>an</u>-o-don).
It looked like a huge bat with leathery wings.
It could glide down from the sky and with its long bill
snatch fish from the sea waves.
It lived seventy million years ago.

Many other strange animals lived long ago.
Archelon (ar-ka-lon) was the largest turtle
that ever lived.
It was twelve feet long — about the size of a car.
It weighed six thousand pounds!
It had a hooked beak and huge flippers.
Its bones were found in South Dakota.
Twenty-five million years ago,
South Dakota was covered by water.
Archelon lived in that inland sea.

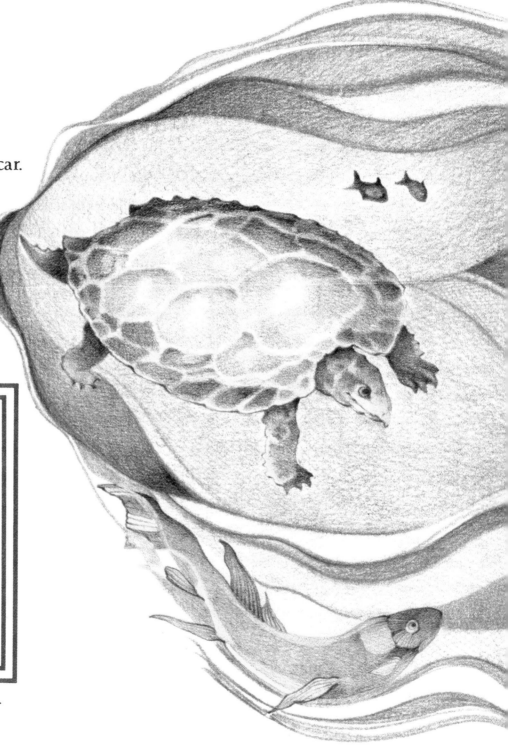

Length of VW car—13 feet.

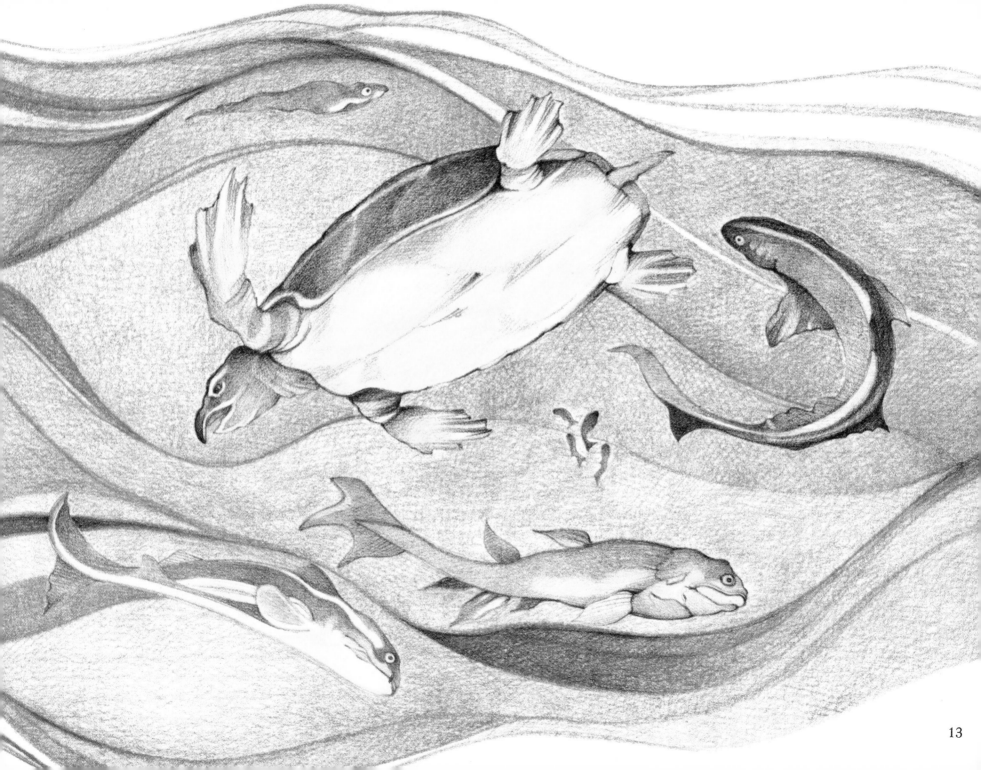

Here is another strange animal —
a colossal crocodile (<u>crok</u>-o-dile)
longer than a school bus!
Two hundred million years ago, it roamed
swamps and riverbanks all over the world.
It snapped up any animal that came close to shore.
The largest crocodiles today are dwarfs
compared to the fifty-foot body of this animal.

The *archaeopteryx* (ar-kay-<u>op</u>-ter-icks) looked like
a small dinosaur with feathers.
Scientists think it might have been the first bird
ever to exist. It lived one hundred forty million years ago.
It had a tail and rounded wings.
It also had teeth in its jaws. No bird today has teeth.
Did it fly? Did it glide from tree to tree?
Scientists are not sure.
Archaeopteryx may be the missing link
between scaly reptiles and feathered birds.

Six horns on its head!
Here is an animal as strange as any dinosaur.
Its name was *uintatherium* (yoo-in-ta-<u>ther</u>-ee-um).
It was about the size of an elephant.
Its sharp teeth made it look scary, but scientists
have discovered that it ate only plants.
Sixty million years ago, it thundered over the plains
of the American West.

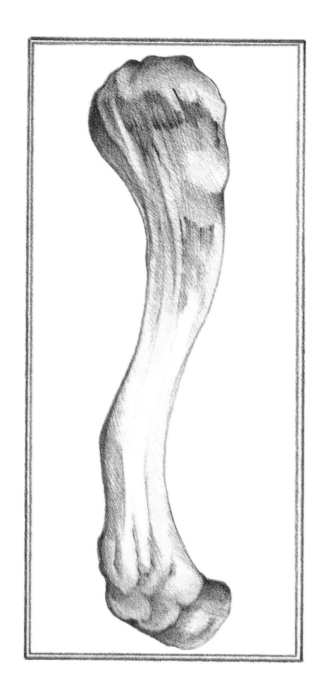

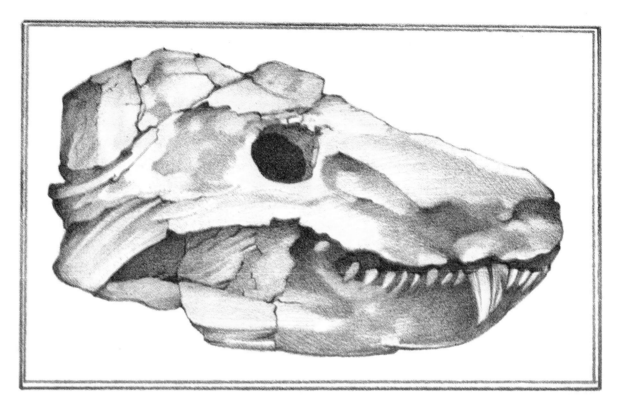

Huge animals once lived in South America.
About one hundred years ago,
a scientist named Charles Darwin found their bones.
Other scientists put the bones together
so they could see what these animals looked like.

One of these animals was a giant land *sloth* (slawth).
It looked like a great hairy bear.
It was as tall as a telephone pole.
From its flat teeth, you can see that it ate plants.
Scientists think it pushed over trees
to get at the leaves in the upper branches.
There are no such sloths alive in the world today.
The last giant sloths died one million years ago.
But we can find their relatives
in Central and South America —
the slow-moving sloths
that hang upside down in the treetops there.

This animal was called the "stabbing cat"
because it had enormous teeth shaped like daggers.
It used its teeth to stab and kill its prey.
Fifty thousand years ago, many cats of this kind
walked into tar pits and were trapped there.
Their flesh decayed, but their bones remained.

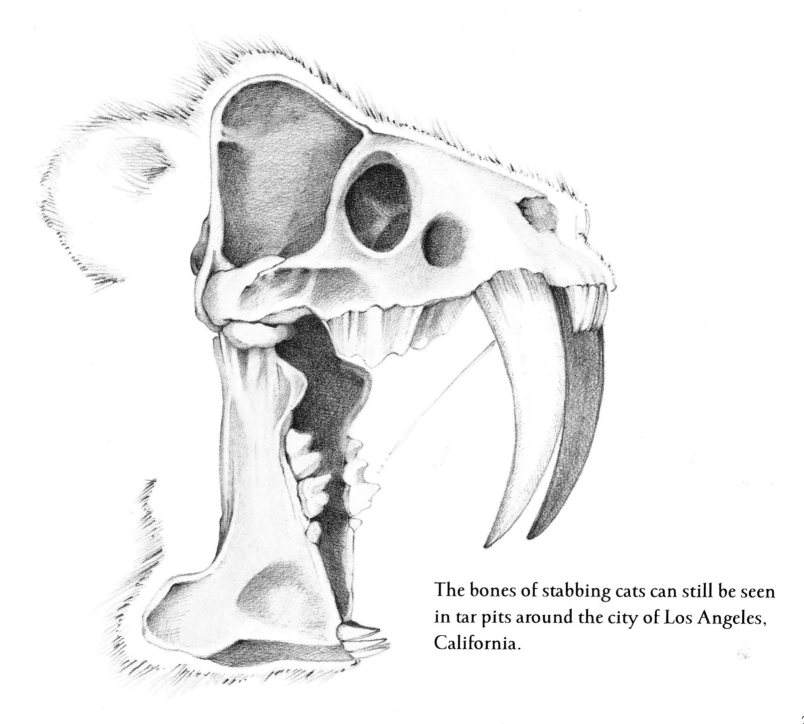

The bones of stabbing cats can still be seen in tar pits around the city of Los Angeles, California.

About twenty million years ago,
there lived an animal called the *camelus* (<u>ca</u>-me-lus).
It looked like a camel with a very long neck.
No wonder it was called the "giraffe camel."
Like the giraffe we know today,
this camel fed on the leaves of trees.
Did it have a hump? We don't know.
Nothing is left that can give us an answer.

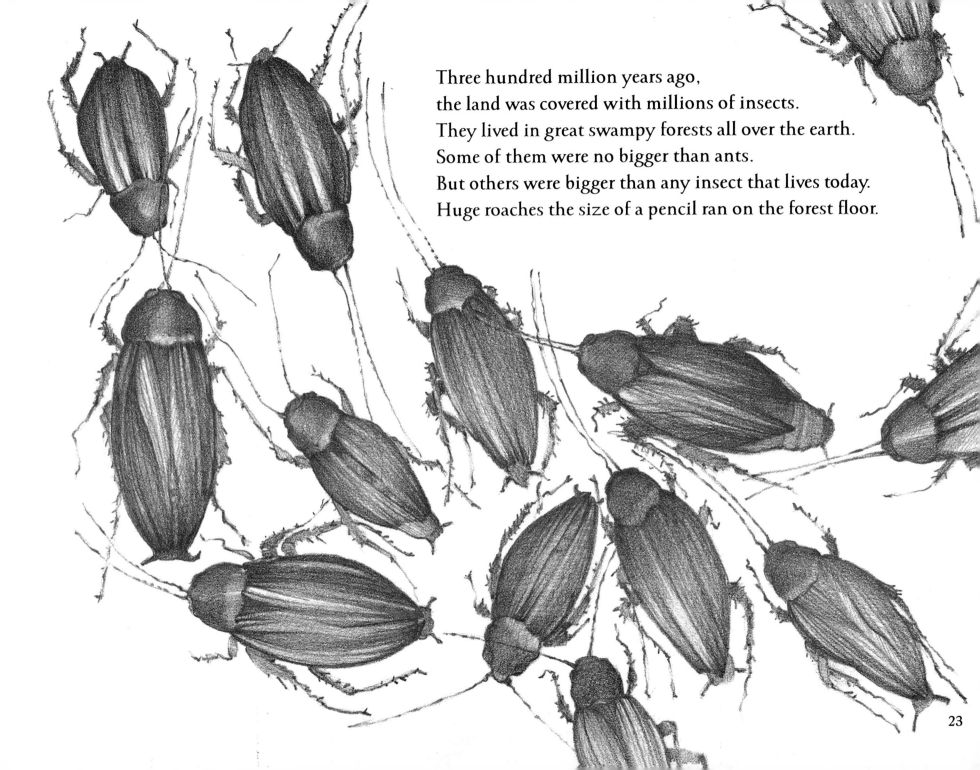

Three hundred million years ago,
the land was covered with millions of insects.
They lived in great swampy forests all over the earth.
Some of them were no bigger than ants.
But others were bigger than any insect that lives today.
Huge roaches the size of a pencil ran on the forest floor.

23

Giant-sized dragonflies flew overhead like kites.

In later times — forty to fifty million years ago —
there were great pine forests.
Sticky resin oozed from the cracks in the trees,
and many small insects got caught in it.
When the resin hardened, it turned into clear amber.
When we look inside that amber today,
the insects seem as though
they might still be alive.
But of course they are not.

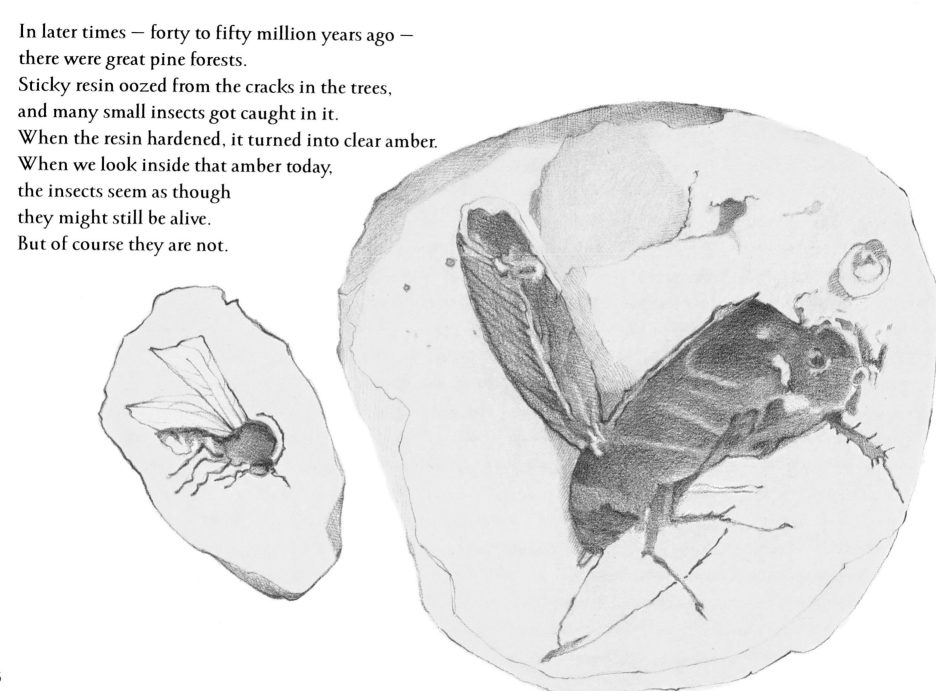

In 1922, scientists went on an expedition
to the Gobi Desert in Asia.
There they found the bones of a giant animal
that lived twenty to thirty million years ago.
It looked like a rhinoceros without horns.
Today all rhinoceroses have horns.
It was called the *baluchitherium* (ba-<u>loo</u>-ki-<u>ther</u>-ee-um),
or the "Beast of Baluchistan" (Ba-<u>loo</u>-ki-stan),
because its bones were first found
in Baluchistan, Mongolia.

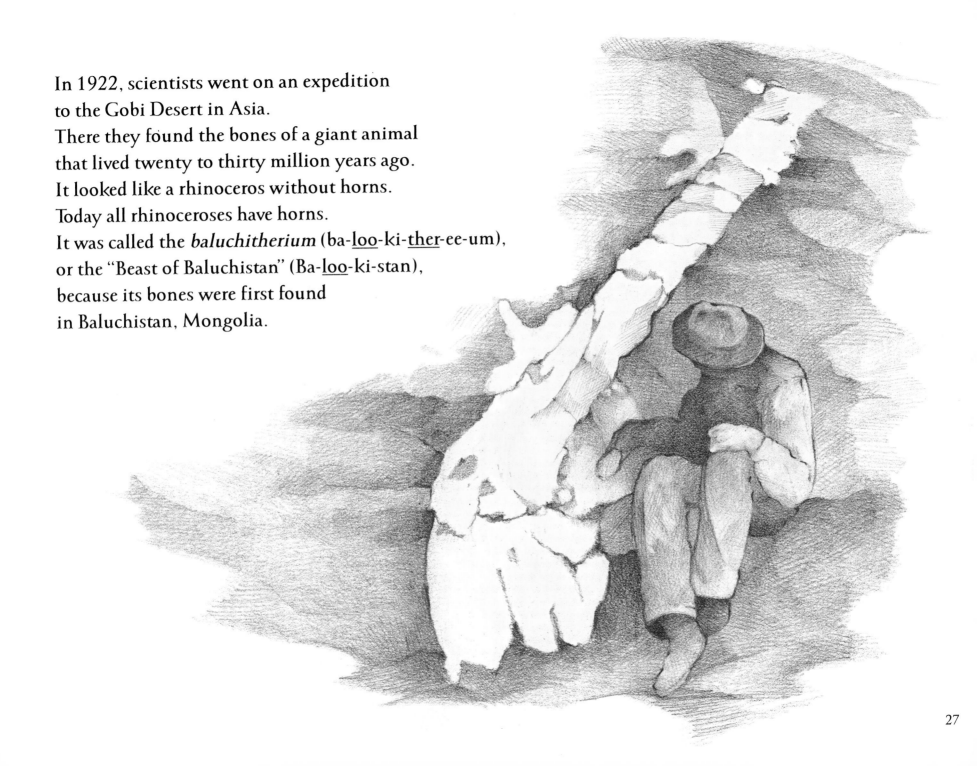

It was the size of a small house.
It measured thirty-four feet from nose to tail,
and eighteen feet from the ground up.
It traveled in herds across the plains of Asia.
It was taller than a giraffe, but much heavier.
Like a giraffe, it could reach the highest branches.
It had only to stretch out its neck to eat twigs,
leaves, and flowers twenty feet off the ground.

Just over three hundred years ago, there lived
a funny-looking bird called the *dodo* (doh-doh).
It was as big as a turkey.
It waddled as it walked on short, stubby legs.
Its curved beak was nine inches long.
Its wings were so short that it could not fly.
It lived on islands in the Indian Ocean.
When ships stopped there, sailors killed the dodo for food.
They left pigs and rats that ate up
the dodos' eggs and their young.
Now there are no dodos anywhere in the world.

UINTATHERIUM

ARCHELON

ARCHAEOPTERYX

BEAST OF BALUCHISTAN

STABBING CAT

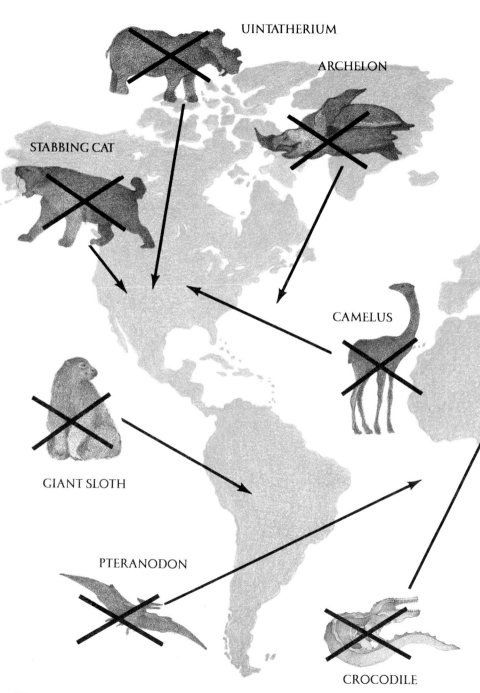

CAMELUS

GIANT SLOTH

PTERANODON

CROCODILE

DODO

All the animals in this book lived a long time ago.
You cannot see them anywhere in the world today
because they have died out.
They are *extinct*.
Right now, many kinds of animals are disappearing.
Some of these animals may never be found again.
They may also become extinct.

People spread over the land.
They cut down forests.
They build roads where only animals lived before.

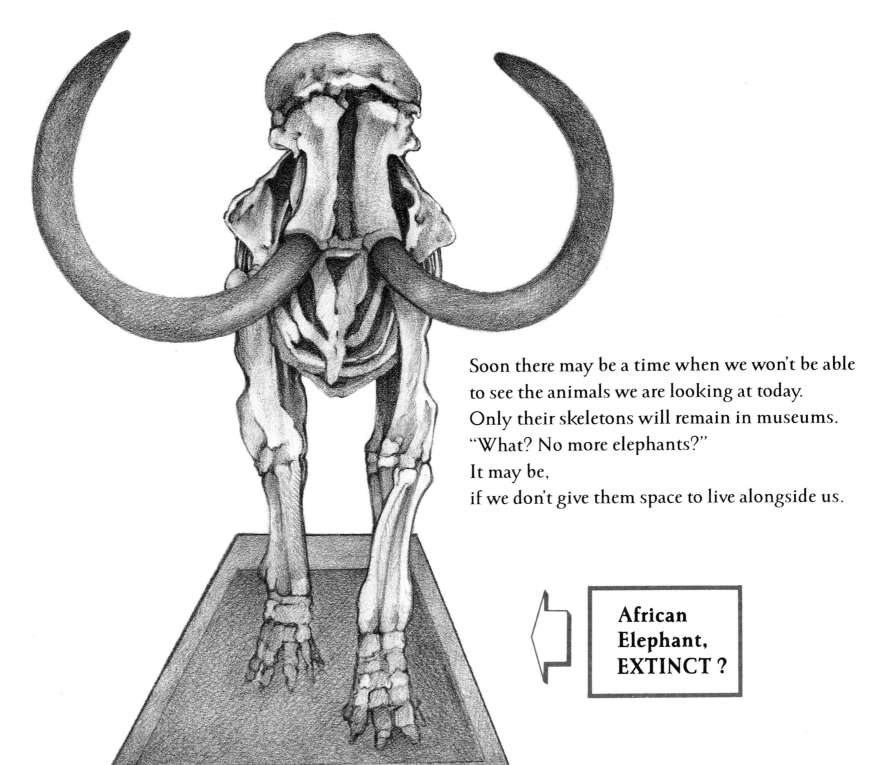

Soon there may be a time when we won't be able
to see the animals we are looking at today.
Only their skeletons will remain in museums.
"What? No more elephants?"
It may be,
if we don't give them space to live alongside us.

**African
Elephant,
EXTINCT ?**

List of Animals in This Book

Page Number	Scientific Name	Approximate Dates of Existence (years B.C. except where noted)	Habitat
Front Jacket	Pteranodon	70 million	World
	Archelon	25 million	North American oceans
Back Jacket	Dinichthys	395 million	North America and Europe
page 1	Anchisaurus	200 million	World
page 2	Smilodon (Stabbing Cat)	50,000	North American Southwest
page 3	Pteranodon (see front jacket)		
	Hypsilophodon	120-140 million	North America and Europe
page 4	Fabrosaurus	140 million	Africa
page 5	Spinosaurus	100 million	Europe, Africa, North America
	Stegosaurus	140 million	North America
page 6	Brontosaurus	140 million	North America
page 7	Camptosaurus	140 million	Western Europe, N.W. America
pages 8-9	Cladoselache	345 million	World oceans
	Climatius	345 million	Northern oceans
	Bothriolepis	345 million	World oceans
	Pleiosaur	65-100 million	World oceans
	Cheirolepis	345 million	World oceans
	Cephalaspis	345 million	Northern oceans
pages 10-11	Pteranodon (see front jacket)		
pages 12-13	Archelon (see front jacket)		
	Dipterus (see pp. 8-9)		
	Cladoselache (see pp. 8-9)		
pages 12-13	Eusthenopteron	345 million	Northern oceans
	Cladoselache (see above)		
page 14	Giant Crocodile	140 million	Europe, Africa
page 16	Archaeopteryx	140 million	Europe
page 17	Uintatherium	60 million	North America
page 19	Megatherium (Giant Land Sloth)	1 million	North American Southwest
page 20	Smilodon (see p. 2)		
page 22	Camelus	20 million	North America
page 23	Early Cockroaches	300 million	World
pages 24-26	Early Dragonflies	40-50 million	World
	Early Beetles	40-50 million	World
pages 27-28	Baluchitherium (Beast of Baluchistan)	20-30 million	Asian deserts
page 29	Dodo	17th Century A.D.	Islands in the Indian Ocean
page 32	Pteranodon (see front jacket)		

Animals are listed from left to right.